Juice Recipes

Juice Recipes for Weight Loss and Health

A Weight Loss Juicing Book with Tips about Sugar

Peggy Annear

⊛

- VISIT THE AUTHOR'S PAGE -
WWW.AMAZON.COM/AUTHOR/PEGGY-ANNEAR

ISBN-13: 978-1499745443

ISBN-10: 1499745443

Table of Contents

The Benefits of Homemade Juice

J **uices are one of the best ways to get nutrients into your body fast!** Juices are easily digested and they feed our body's cells efficiently. They usually taste amazing too! Fruit juices tend to supply the body with more vitamins, whereas vegetables tend to supply the body with more minerals. The fun of juicing is in its flexibility. You can add particular things to your recipe that you think you may be lacking in your diet. Be creative!

The freshness and ripeness of fruit and vegetables play a role in how much health benefit we get from our juicing recipes. A general rule of thumb is the richer or deeper color of a fruit or vegetable, the more nutrient dense it is. The quality of soil where they were grown also plays an important role, so local market gardens are a fabulous place to source your foods. Even better of course is growing them yourself in healthy fertile soils. Wherever possible grow or buy organic products that are free of chemical residues.

Drinking homemade healthy juices in place of high sugar, high fat foods will help you lose weight. This works for many people. However, a juice diet alone is not a balanced diet long term and should not be what you aim for with regards to optimal health and nutrition. Sometimes particular problems with digestion or other ailments however can benefit from a quick intake of juices and nothing else very short term to restore the body's health quickly. But **using juices one or two times a day to get beneficial nutrient, power boosting properties into your diet really helps general health**. It's a quick and effective way to get much needed vitamins, minerals and enzymes straight into your blood stream.

Adding some ice cubes or crushed ice can bring any drink to life! This is especially true of the green juices when they aren't very sweet in taste. Once you make your juice, pour into a glass or jug with ice and see the difference. You can refrigerate or freeze any juice leftovers. Another option is to place into ice cube trays and use later.

CऄƏO

JUICE RECIPES FOR WEIGHT LOSS

Your aim for weight loss is to eat foods that are low in calories but high in nutritional content. This way you will beat the cravings and find it easier to stay on track to meet your weight loss goals. There are certain combinations of foods that actively work to help you in your pursuit of a healthier body and this one is sure to enliven your blood cells, energize your digestion and give you a healthy glow. **Juice recipe ingredients that are great for weight loss include broccoli, kale, parsley, spinach and Brussels sprouts.** These are packed full of nutrition, and have the green chlorophyll benefit. **Foods such as beets, cabbage, cauliflower and capsicum peppers are less common due to their strong flavor. Of course citrus, blueberries, celery, apples, carrots, melons and strawberries are all popular because of their sweeter taste.** These can be used to offset any unpleasant tasting juices. Remember the importance of drinking plenty of water each day!

Keeping your metabolism ticking over will keep your energy levels up. Making a juice for morning or afternoon tea may be best for you. Observe how your body feels and responds after drinking juices.

When You Aren't Hungry

Juices can help if you don't feel hungry, you feel unwell, or just have a sore stomach and don't feel like eating. It actually takes the body effort to digest food, so if you don't want to eat, you may want to skip a meal, just have a light juice to go easy on your body.

Vegetables full of fibre and nutrients should play a large part in our food consumption. If you want to be strict, eating about 6 vegetables, 2 fruits, 1 protein and 1 starch is suggested by many nutritionists. By eating a variety of different foods, this will help get a nutritional balance. Try to eat your fruits early in the day and eat plenty of vegetables with lunch, dinner and snacks. Don't overcook your vegetables and other foods as this can deplete nutritional value. Another way to keep a "happy stomach" is by drinking about 8 glasses of fresh water daily and not to over eat! I drink a glass first thing in the morning before breakfast to fire the kidneys up!

Leafy Green Power

Adding plenty of freshly juiced greens to your diet gives you an abundance of beneficial nutrients. They are usually rich in Chlorophyll and calcium amongst other things. Leafy greens like wheatgrass, kale, dandelion greens, alfalfa and spinach being some of the most popular. Chlorophyll is an excellent blood cleanser. This helps maintain healthy cells and cleans the blood. Being loaded with antioxidants, greens are beneficial for boosting our immune system and wonderful for weight loss. Read more about leafy greens here.

Try to source organically grown fruits and vegetables that haven't been sprayed with chemicals if possible. If you aren't peeling them, then wash to remove any possible chemical residue that may be present.

Juicing machines grind the fruits and vegetables then extract the juice from the pulp. You will need an electric juicer that is right for your needs. If you intend on juicing nuts and harder vegetables, then don't scrimp on a cheap machine, as it may lead to disappointment because it just isn't up to the job! There are a variety of juicers on the market.

Some separate most foods, some work better in combination with blended ingredients.

Water is Important

Drinking plenty of water each day has many benefits. It hydrates your body's cells, it flushes toxins out of your system, it helps you feel full, it prevents constipation and it is good for your skin. Try to drink around 8 glasses a day! I drink my first one in the morning when I get up to help fire up the kidneys!

Fibre is Important

For very similar reasons to water, fibre also helps our body work like a well oiled engine. Eat your fruits and vegetables!

ଓ୫୦

GREEN CLEANSING RECIPES

Green vegetable and herb juices help clean the blood and lymphatic system. Juices rich in Chlorophyll have a wonderful cleansing effect and other elimination processes that go on in our bodies. Green vegetable juices build a good red blood count which in turn gets more oxygen into your tissues to aid in cell health. As you know, if you feel well and full of energy you are more likely to lose weight and want to be more active. It's a chain reaction and a bit like an "anti aging" boost! Greens are wonderful antioxidants and also help control calcium in the body, assisting in healing, feeding the "good" bacteria in the stomach which helps clean the bowel. When you feel energetic and healthy it will be easier to lose weight. **As you can see, green juices really are a power house for our health!**

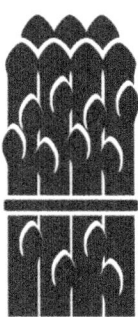

People often want the nutritional benefits of a green smoothie, but struggle to drink a thick smoothie, so this is where juicing is excellent. If you want, you can still blend certain foods such as nuts or bananas in a blender then add them to your juicer recipe. This way blending and juicing is very flexible and can work well together...the sky is the limit. If you need to add more sweetener, add some honey, maple syrup of Stevia, not sugar.

My Sugar Free Recipes book has more information about the problems with processed sugars, how to read food labels and 52 sugar free and carb free recipes for weight loss.

Mix up the foods you include in your diet. **Variety is very important** to get a wide range of nutrients and minerals into our bodies for optimal health. Eat a variety of healthy foods. Unfortunately cooking removes about 50% of protein, so you may want to eat some raw foods regularly as this is will not only boost your protein levels but also your nutrient intake. Many goodies are packed inside the skins or just under the skins of fruits and vegetables.

CR&O

FRUIT & VEGETABLE WASH

You will need to wash your fruits and vegetables if they aren't organic to remove any chemical residue. This will also remove any dirt that may be lingering. This is why home grown veggies, herbs and fruits are so good - you don't have to worry about quality control!

Ingredients:

1 cup vinegar
1 cup water
2 Tbsp lemon juice
1 Tbsp baking soda

Directions:

Place all ingredients into a large bowl and mix together. After all the fizzing from the baking soda is finished, pour the mix into a spray bottle. Spray your produce and leave it stand for at least a few minutes before washing off thoroughly.

CBEO

JUICING TIPS

Juicing Tips for Beginners - These are important!

- Use organic, home grown and fresh produce wherever possible.

- Popular fruit juice bases can include apple, grape, pineapple, cherries, pomegranate and berries.

- Popular vegetable juice bases can include tomato, celery, carrot and spinach, kale and other mixed greens. Spinach and Kale are highly alkaline and wonderful for sugar detox!

- If desired, use the leftover pulp in cooking, cakes or muffins.

- Stir in some unsweetened almond milk, skinny milk, coconut milk or water if desired after juicing.

- A tip about juices for beginners; slowly introduce a few small pieces of vegetables into your juice to begin with! We don't want that "yuk" effect if you go from fruit juices straight over to a full green juice. Gradual introduction and moderation is the key for developing the taste buds.

- Chop fruits and vegetables into about 2 - 3 inch square pieces, or to fit YOUR chute. Read manual instructions.

- For best result, juice less dense, or softer fruits and vegetables first followed by the harder varieties.

- Apple and cucumber peels are best left on for their high fibre and nutritional content. So wash thoroughly and try to source organic!

- You can't juice bananas due to their structure (no juice) but you can juice their peels...they are good for you being rich in serotonin, which is a natural anti depressant.

- Bananas and avocados can't be juiced, but If you want to add them, blend first as a smoothie, then add to your juice.

- Be creative and add variety by mixing juicer drinks with blended smoothies.

- When juicing for young children, gradually introduce pieces of vegetables into fruit juices to be sure they like it.

- Wash fruits and vegetables before juicing to remove any chemical residue.

- Drink juice soon after being made because it keeps more nutrients.

- It's okay to add powdered supplements to your juice; e.g. spirulina etc.

- If you juice eggplant for it's antioxidant effect, leave the skin on, but juice it when fresh because the skins get bitter with age.

- Bunch up leafy greens together before putting them through the juicer, alternating with other fruits or vegetables for a better juicing result, and to reduce clogging.

- For a thinner juice, consider base liquids such as orange, grapefruit or pineapple juice.

- Kiwi fruit can be juiced with the skins on for the antioxidant and nutritional benefits. If it's too tart, try the golden variety.

- Lemon peels are full of super-flavonoids helping reduce bad cholesterol. However, they are strong on the tummy, so juice only about 1/2 peel a day. When you cut lemons up, just leave a little peel on. Too much tends to give a bitter taste.

- As a general rule of thumb; peel oranges, lemons, grapefruits, and especially pineapple, pumpkin and cantaloupes. In other words, super hard skins.

- Watermelons can be juiced as is, just cut into chunks. Some prefer to remove skin but the rind contains citrulline, which has an antioxidant effect. Seeds aren't a problem.

- Juice mango skins with caution as SOME people have skin allergy problems with them.

- Hard skins on vegetables like pumpkin and pineapple are much too hard to juice, so peel.

- Vegetables should be incorporated into your juices for nutrient value and sugar balance.

- If you drink ALL fruit juices ALL the time, this may increase your weight because of the possible high sugar content.

- If juices are too strong or bitter, particularly green juices, add apple or carrot, or pineapple or watermelon.

- Parsley helps neutralize the odor of garlic.

- Some like to juice a lemon separately and add to juicer recipe afterwards for slowing the oxidization process of juice.

- If you are adding apples, add them last if not drinking juice straight away.

- This may seem obvious, but many do not do it - read through the information provided with your juicer to become familiar with exactly how your machine works, how to get the most out of it, as well as the recipes probably included.

HEALING & WEIGHT LOSS FOODS

FOODS FOR SPECIFIC HEALTH ISSUES

While many fruits and vegetables have a variety of helpful effects on our bodies, this is just a snapshot of a few, and some of the benefits they hold.

- Broccoli, Spinach & Cauliflower support weight loss because they are high in folates, which help cell production.
- Cabbage is good for stomach health and treating peptic ulcers. It is also high in folates.
- Leafy green vegetable juice can help it treating leg ulcers and sores.
- Beets are good for cleansing the liver, gall bladder and bowel.
- Raspberries and blackberries are good for weight loss due to being quite low in sugars and high in vitamin C.
- Natural sweeteners can be used such as soaked dates, raisins, and prunes. Date sugar, maple syrup, carob powder and raw honey are also good. Stevia is also a popular sugar alternative.
- Apple and pineapple juice are good to help cover up a "yucky" taste.
- Cayenne pepper is good for circulation.
- Alfalfa is good for bowel health.
- Anise (herb) will help reduce gas in the stomach.
- Citrus fruits, and any fruit/veg high in ascorbic acid help boost the immune system and fight cancer.
- Carrots contain beta carotene which help fight infection and cancer.
- Coriander (cilantro) is good for the heart and the digestive system.

- Dandelion is a mild diuretic.
- Echinacea is a good detoxifying agent for cleaning the lymphatic system.
- Figs and prunes are a natural laxative.
- Ginger helps improve digestion and circulation.
- Grapes are a good blood purifier.
- Kale is high in calcium and good for our teeth and bones.
- Lemons, oranges and grapefruit help eliminate catarrh, and boost immune system.
- Lentils are a muscle building food.
- Mangoes are good for the intestines.
- Milk (cows) is a complete protein.
- Lettuce can slow digestion, but is good for insomnia.
- Parsley is a tonic for the kidneys and blood vessels.
- Mint is good to help cover a "yucky" taste and also good for digestion.
- Pineapple is a good source of manganese and vitamin C, great for the blood and digestion.
- Pomegranate is good for urinary problems and is a detox blood cleanser.
- Papaya is good for intestinal disorders.
- Radish is good for catarrh.
- Sage is a good "wake up" herb and also good for the sinuses.
- Spinach is great raw in drinks, but don't overdo it because it contains oxalic acid.
- Thyme helps alleviate headaches, asthma and cold symptoms associated with the upper respiratory system.
- Watermelon is good for the kidneys and is a blood cooler.
- Watercress helps eliminate fluids from the body because it is high in potassium.
- Wheatgrass is high in Indole which helps prevent cancer. It is high in many beneficial enzymes.

LOW SUGAR FRUITS

Now you know why berry smoothies are popular for weight **loss!** They are low in sugar, taste amazing and contain detoxifying enzymes. Lemons, limes, raspberries, blackberries, cranberries and rhubarb are all good too.

HIGH SUGAR FRUITS

While eating fruit is full of nutrition and better than high calorie loaded foods, eat these fruits in moderation when first trying to drop the pounds quickly. Over ripe fruit often has more sugar than under ripe.

A Snapshot of high sugar fruits: Grapes, Tangerines, Cherries, Pomegranates, Mangoes, Figs, Bananas and dried fruits.

JTION   CAUTION

ON   CAUTION

THE LOW FAT WEIGHT LOSS MYTH

It **might be okay in choosing unsweetened milks such as almond milk for example, but you will need to read labels when shopping because low fat products can be loaded with sugars to put some "taste" back in.** A classic example of this is in foods such as low fat yoghurts, low fat creams, ice cream and cookies. This from WebMD.com is an interesting read which sums it up well. So read sugar and carb labels when shopping, not just fat.

"When you read the labels on foods in your supermarket, it's no surprise that you find plenty of sugar in products like cake mix, ice cream, jelly, cookies, and soda. But it can be downright shocking to see 12 grams of sugar in bottled pasta sauce or barbecue sauce -- and even more so to find 50 grams of sugar in a healthy-sounding bottled tea! So how much exactly is a gram of sugar? One teaspoon of granulated sugar equals 4 grams of sugar. To put it another way, 16 grams of sugar in a product is equal to about 4 teaspoons of granulated sugar.

Keep in mind, though, that the grams of sugar listed on the nutrition information label includes natural sugars from fruit (fructose) and milk (lactose) as well as added sweeteners like refined sugar or high-fructose corn syrup. That's why the label on a carton of regular low-fat milk says there's 13 grams of sugar per cup. And that's why the grams of sugar per serving in Raisin Bran (or any cereal with raisins or other dried fruit) seem unexpectedly high"

In addition to this, **carbohydrates are the body's main source of energy and during digestion, sugar which is simple carbohydrates, and starches which are complex carbohydrates, break down into**

blood sugar also known as glucose. Consuming too much food that is high in carbohydrates quickly can spike blood sugar levels which may cause problems over time. Monitoring and maintaining carbohydrate intake is key to blood sugar control.

Potato is a classic example. It has under 1g of sugar per 100 g, but has about 20g of carbs. Lentils have about 2g of sugar but 60g of carbs! So does this mean we must never eat potatoes...I'd say heck no unless you have a specific dietary reason. We live in a modern world so just have a few on occasion, not a plate full at once! **Think in terms of balance and moderation.** Talk to your dietician or doctor if you have concerns and want to learn more.

⊰⊱

HOW TO READ LABELS

This may be useful for people trying to lose weight. Learn to read the labels on foods.

Locate the "Nutritional Information" on the food packaging. Look for "Total Carbohydrates" and "Sugars" as both these will be indicated there. If serving size is difficult to compare, analyse per 100g.

WHAT IS AN ACCEPTABLE AMOUNT OF SUGAR?

- High – over 22g of total sugars per 100g
- Low – 5g of total sugars or less per 100g

*If the amount of sugars per 100g is between these figures, then that is a medium level of sugars.

*The sugar amount in the nutrition label is the total amount of sugars in the food. It includes added sugars and sugars from fruit and milk. Eggs have around 1g of sugar per 100g, depending on if they are cooked.

CHECK TOTAL CARBOHYDRATES

Carbs are the complex part of sugar so they need to be watched as well. For example quinoa may have only 0.9g of sugar per 100g, but has 64g of total carbs! It is also however high in fibre, so this is where a balanced diet full of a variety of natural foods in your best option for health and weight loss. Moderation is the key when eating high carb or high sugar foods. In saying that, all "junk" foods need to be removed altogether as they have virtually no nutritional value whatsoever!

WHAT IS AN ACCEPTABLE AMOUNT OF CARBS?

As a guide, if you eat about 2,000 calories a day, you should consume about 250g of complex carbohydrates per day. That's about 1/8th.

Here is an example of food labels; one giving stats for Serving Size, the other per100g: Always note the sugars and total carbs.

Nutrition Facts

Serving Size 1 Bar (85g)
Servings Per Container 4

Amount Per Serving

Calories 170   Calories from Fat 50

	% Daily Value *
Total Fat 6g	**9%**
Saturated Fat 4g	**19%**
Trans Fat 0g	
Polyunsaturated Fat 0.5g	
Monounsaturated Fat 1g	
Cholesterol 13mg	**4%**
Sodium 83mg	**3%**
Total Carbohydrate 33g	**11%**
Dietary Fiber 4g	**16%**
Sugar 25g	
Protein 3g	

Vitamin A 110%	•	Vitamin C 2%
Calcium 10%	•	Iron 3%

*Percent Daily Values are based on a 2,000 calorie diet. Your daily values may be higher or lower depending on your calorie needs.

	Calories	2,000	2,500
Total Fat	Less than	65g	80g
Sat Fat	Less than	20g	25g
Cholesterol	Less than	300mg	300mg
Sodium	Less than	2,400mg	2,400mg
Total Carbohydrate		300g	375g
Dietary Fiber		25g	30g

Calories per gram:
Fat 9   •   Carbohydrate 4   •   Protein 4

Nutrient	Per Serv	Per 100g
Calories (kcal)	130.85	307.7
Calories from Fat (kcal)	28.66	67.39
Fat (g)	3.22	7.58
Saturated Fat (g)	0.61	1.44
Trans Fatty Acid (g)	0.01	0.01
Cholesterol (mg)	0	0
Carbohydrates (g)	21.8	51.27
Dietary Fiber (g)	1.97	4.63
Total Sugars (g)	0.74	1.74
Protein (g)	3.44	8.09
Mono Fat (g)	0.53	1.25

VEGETABLES LOW IN SUGAR

Here is a snapshot of vegetables that are lower in sugars. There are loads of them! Beets and carrots are on the high side, so use these as a sweetener to your vegetable juices.

Alfalfa sprouts
Asparagus
Avocado
Bamboo sprouts
Bean sprouts
Beet greens
Bell pepper (sweet green)
Broccoli
Brussels sprouts
Cabbage - all kinds
Cauliflower
Celery
Collard greens
Cucumber
Dandelion greens
Eggplant
Endive
Escarole
Garlic
Green bean, string 3.3g
Kale 1.2g
Leek
Lettuce (all kinds)
Mung bean sprouts
Mushroom
Mustard greens
Okra

Onion
Radish
Arugula
Shallot
Spaghetti squash
Spinach 0.4g
Squash (summer)
Swiss chard
Tomato
Turnip greens
Watercress
Zucchini

CB80

SKINNY PINK JUICE

Ingredients:

1 pink grapefruit, peeled (try to keep some white on)
2 cups raspberries, blueberries, blackberries or 1 orange

Directions:

Juice together. This is good for weight loss first thing in the day. It is very low in calories, however the natural sugars help reduce appetite. It is also rich in flavonoids, especially if you leave the (albido) white peel in. Berries are great when trying to lose weight. An antioxidant yummy drink!

CAN'T BEET IT JUICE

Ingredients:

3 medium carrots
½ raw beet, including greens if desired
1 medium apple
2 large stalks of celery
A small bunch of parsley

Directions:

Simply cut the ingredients to a manageable size for your machine,
juice, pour into a chilled glass and give it a stir. Find a nice cozy spot
to recline in and let the magic of this power combo do its thing.
Bottoms Up!

Low Cal Cantaloupe Juice

Ingredients:

1/2 cantaloupe with skin, chopped
1 cup strawberries (or kiwi fruit)

Directions:

Juice alternately between both ingredients. Great for the immune system and weight loss due to being low in calories. This is great put into the freezer and made into ice blocks. Kiwi fruit makes a nice change to this recipe and gives it that nice zing!

SKINNY MINI GINGER JUICE

Ingredients:

1 piece ginger, 1/2 - 3/4 inch
2 green apples, chopped
1 small carrot, chopped
1/2 packed cup beet greens, chopped
1/4 cucumber, chopped
1 lemon, peeled

Directions:

Chop vegetables and apples, peel lemon (can leave on 1/4 of the skin for added nutrients) Add the ginger to juice. Enliven your blood cells and energize your digestion. Great nutrient dense low calorie ingredients for weight loss.

V8 WEIGHT LOSS JUICE

Ingredients:

1 stick celery
1/2 small cucumber
1 cup packed baby spinach leaves
1/2 cup curly leaf or Italian parsley
1/2 ripe pear
1/4 ripe papaya with seeds removed
1/2 green apple
a small 1/2 tsp size piece of ginger

Directions:

Chop and juice by adding parsley and spinach - alternating with the other ingredients. Parsley is loaded with antioxidants like luteolin. This helps prevent the oxidation of cells. Great energizer for weight loss, plus packed full of vitamins and nutrients.

FAT BLASTER

Ingredients:

2 carrots
1/2 cup kale
1/2 cup baby spinach leaves or broccoli
1/4 cucumber
3 celery sticks
1 piece of ginger (about 1/2 tsp)
2 small tomatoes
1/2 lemon or lime
1 cup blueberries
1 apple

Directions:

Chop carrot, kale, cucumber, celery, tomato, citrus and apple roughly.
Push through juicer alternating as you go.
Blueberries contain polyphenols which are great for weight loss. This
juice is packed full of nutrition!

Pomegranate Power Juice

Ingredients:

1 large pomegranate
2 large carrots, chopped
½ stick of celery
1 peeled and cored green or red apple (red are sweeter than green)

Directions:

Push the red seeds out of the shell and carefully place into your juicer. You may want to do this over a larger bowl to ensure you don't loose too much juice. Put the other ingredients into your juicer and juice away. Drink straight away or chill for a half hour for a refreshingly cold tangy drink.

GREEN DETOX JUICE

Ingredients:

5 small carrots, chopped
1/2 cup wheatgrass
1 sprig parsley
2 sticks of celery
1/2 beet, with top
1 large apple, chopped

Directions:

Push the parsley and wheatgrass through the juicer alternately with the
carrot. Now alternate the apple, celery and beet. This is a nutrient
dense drink packed full of healthy chlorophyll and antioxidants.
Wheatgrass is high in Indole which helps prevent cancer. It is high in
many beneficial enzymes.

COOL AS A CUCUMBER

There is something joyful about placing a few simple ingredients into the juicer and drinking the cooling, soothing and refreshing elixir. Cucumber, apple and celery – a combination helpful in aiding weight loss and generally making you feel good!

Ingredients:

1 whole cucumber, chopped
1 large green apple, chopped
1 – 2 sticks of celery

Directions:

Simply wash, cut and core ingredients, place into juicer and juice. For a little twist, add ½ a pomegranate to give it a wonderful sour jolt to enliven your system!

CINNAMON CIRCULATION BOOSTER

Ingredients:

1/2 inch piece of ginger
1/2 tsp cinnamon
6 small apples, chopped

Directions:

Juice the ginger and apple. Pour into glasses, divide the cinnamon
between the two and stir in. This warming concoction is great before
bed time on a winter's night. The ginger and cinnamon are good for
your liver too. Ginger is also known to help improve digestion and
circulation.

BEE POLLEN ENERGY DRINK

This is pure and simple drink, but bursting full of energy before you exercise!

Directions:

Add a **heaped Tbsp of honeybee pollen to a glass of any natural fruit or vegetable juice.** Serve immediately.

Honeybee pollen is known for improving allergies and benefits to the heart. *If you haven't taken honey bee pollen before, be cautious because some people are sensitive to it. Try just a little first. This is a great afternoon "pick me up" or pre- workout booster.

Salad in a Glass

Don't like eating your greens? Why not try juicing them? Sure, it's weird but the amount of antioxidants you can get in a salad juice is well worth the effort and your body will thank you. Try juicing these ingredients and of course, alter the quantities a little to taste. A smooth running body helps improve energy levels, hence motivation to keep active.

Ingredients:

1 cucumber
1 whole lemon, peeled and quartered
1 medium scallion (onion)
A handful of parsley (the flat leaf variety has a milder taste and texture)
½ a medium sweet red pepper
3 small whole tomatoes

Directions:

Rinse the cucumber and cut up into chunks. Leave the skin on because this is where the highest nutrient quantity is. Roughly chop a medium onion with a handful of parsley. Wash and chop the pepper and tomatoes and put it all in the juicer. Juice, shake, stir and drink.

ANTIOXIDANT BOK CHOY JUICE

Ingredients:

1 lemon, peeled
1 large or 2 small bok choy (sometimes I add kale or spinach)
1 beet
3 carrots, chopped
3 sticks celery
1 apple, chopped
1/2 cup natural blackcurrant juice, or blackcurrants (optional)

Directions:

Remove and discard the very base from the bok choy. Juice everything leaving the apple till last. Packed full of vitamin C and also great for the skin and liver! Mix up the greens and use whatever you have in the fridge.

LOW CAL TROPICAL PUNCH

Ingredients:

1 papaya (or mango)
1 large fresh, tinned or home made preserved peach
2 passionfruit
150ml orange juice or 1 halved and peeled orange

Serve with ice and a shot of vodka or white rum (optional)

Directions:

Remove papaya or mango seed, chop roughly and feed into juicer.
Add stoned and halved peach and orange. Juice, then pour into glasses
with ice cubes. Mix in passionfruit pulp including seeds and vodka.

BERRY SUPER LUNCH JUICE

Ingredients:

1 orange, peeled and chopped
2 bananas, peeled and blended on their own first
2 dates
A large handful of Swiss chard or spinach
1 cup blackberries or raspberries (a mix of both is even better)
1 kiwi fruit
1/2 cup strawberries
1 cup water

Directions:

Blend the banana separately. Prepare the orange and push the chard through with this. Then add the other ingredients. Mix with the banana to make a super smoothie drink. This juice is a delicious energy booster and wonderful for a weight watchers breakfast or lunch!

"KITCHEN SINK" DETOX JUICE

Ingredients:

1/2 cup baby spinach
2 small carrots, chopped
2 apples, chopped
2 sticks celery, chopped
1 tomato
1/4 cucumber, chopped
1 cup strawberries
1 kiwi fruit
1/4 lemon
1/2 inch piece of ginger
1/2 cup kale

Directions:

Bunch up the leafy greens and feed them through the juicer machine alternately with the other ingredients. This really is a super healthy detox juice packed full of a home grown garden patch! ALMOST everything, including the kitchen sink!

CRAZY CABBAGE JUICE

Ingredients:

1/2 cabbage, chopped with lower stalk removed
2 carrots, chopped
4 celery sticks

Directions:

Juice the cabbage first, then the carrots and celery. Cabbage is good for the stomach and known to help treat peptic ulcers. The carotene rich carrots also give a powerful punch. Can add an apple or some grapes for added sweetness.

CITRUS WEIGHT BUSTER

Ingredients:

2 oranges, peeled and quartered
1/2 grapefruit, peeled
1/2 lemon, peeled but keep about a tsp size of peel (optional)
½ lime, peeled

Directions:

Peel fruits, but keep 1/4 of the lemon peel on for extra cold fighting properties. Lemon peels are also full of super-flavonoids helping reduce bad cholesterol. I find this recipe can be hard on the tummy, so eat something with it, or dilute with water. Refreshing summer time weight loss drink and a soother for winter colds!

SPARKLING HEALTH DRINK

Ingredients:

1 little bunch of parsley or watercress
4 broccoli florets
1/4 pineapple, peeled and chopped
1 in season sweet apple, chopped (1/4 cup strawberries work too)
1/4 - 1/2 cup sparkling mineral water
(can add 1/2 a blended banana for a low GI juice)

Directions:

Bunch up the parsley and feed all ingredients through the juicer alternately together and serve. Mix with sparkling mineral water to taste. A healthy juice full of vitamin C and vital green nutrients, AND it's yummy! You can change up the juice by leaving out the apple and using 1/2 pineapple. You can also leave out the broccoli and use baby spinach leaves.

WEIGHT LOSS TONIC

Ingredients:

4 strawberries
4 broccoli florets
1/4 cup alfalfa sprouts
1 apple, chopped
1 sprig parsley
1/2 cup baby spinach leaves
1 orange, peeled and chopped (leave some of the white on for
vitamins)

Directions:

Juice all ingredients alternately as you go. This is a tasty vitamin
packed favorite in our family. This is an easy, basic juice with the
ingredients usually on hand. You can change it up by substituting
pineapple or pear for the apple sweet balance, or by using kale or
standard spinach instead of baby spinach. Blend in any of the above
veggies or fruits in the picture and see if you like it. Great for
breakfast, lunch or a snack. Blended under ripe banana may be added
with the juice if desired.

KALE POWERADE

Ingredients:

1 cup kale
¾ cup spinach
1 carrot
½ beet, with leaves
1 apple

Directions:

Chop veg and apple into chunks, feed soft and hard ingredients alternatively to juice. Kale is packed full of protein, vitamins and nutrients.

HOT & SPICY JUICE

Ingredients:

1 clove of garlic
1/4 piece of ginger
1/2 cup of freshly picked parsley
1 apple chopped
4 carrots, chopped
1/4 capsicum pepper, chopped or a splash of Tabasco sauce

Directions:

Juice the garlic, parsley and ginger first; alternate feeding them into the juicer. Then juice the apple and carrots. Parsley helps neutralize the garlic odour. The ingredients in this juice are known to help lower cholesterol, having an especially powerful effect when eaten together. In combination with a diet rich in oats, legumes vegetables and fruits you will beaming on your next visit to the doctor. Rev up the circulation with this one!

Easy Apricot Juice

Ingredients:

10 apricots
1 cup unsweetened almond milk

Directions:

Halve apricots and remove stone. Juice, then pour into glasses half way up, top with almond milk and stir. Add a few ice cubes if desired. This one is great when apricots are in season and there is an abundance of them.

GREEN GODDESS CLEANSE

Ingredients:

1 mango
1 orange
1 1/2 cups kale
2 medium sticks of celery
¼ cup fresh parsley
¼ cup fresh mint
small piece fresh ginger (about ¼ tsp)

Directions:

De seed mango, peel orange. Roughly chop and juice all ingredients
alternately. Kale and mango are loaded with nutrition that support your
detox cleanse for weight loss. Ginger helps improve digestion and
circulation.

BERRY HEAVEN

Ingredients:

2 cup strawberries, hulled
1 cup frozen fruit berries, or other fresh berries such as raspberries or cranberries
1 cup milk (250ml) low fat, unsweetened almond or skim milk (optional)

Directions:

Juice the berries. Mix in the milk if desired. Garnish with a sprig of mint.

SWEET RUBY WEIGHT BUSTER

Ingredients:

1½ cups boysenberry / blackberry juice
1 cup boysenberries / blackberries
1 cup blueberries (fresh or frozen)

* This recipe is delicious made into ice pops!

Directions:

Place berries in juicer. Very flexible with proportions. A stunning &
tasty ruby gemmed wonder that's just 74 cals per serve!

CARROT VITALITY JUICE

Ingredients:

5 large carrots
1 apple
1 piece fresh ginger, (about 1/4 tsp)

Directions:

Chop carrots, ginger and apple into chunks. Juice everything. Carrots are a great source of beta-carotene. Converted into vitamin A, they play an essential role in regulating the immune system.

ZESTY LEMON & MELON JUICE

Ingredients:

1½ cups honeydew or rock-melon, tough skin removed
2 kiwi fruit
1/2 lemon, peeled
1 Tbs chopped fresh mint

Directions:

Chop melon and halve kiwi fruit and lemon. Juice alternately. Just 115 cals per serve with a refreshing tart fruity kick! Can stir through 1/2 cup natural yogurt if desired at the end.

SKINNY GREEN TONIC

Ingredients:

1 ripe juicy pear, halved
2 kiwi fruit
1 large cup washed baby spinach leaves or kale, roughly chopped

Directions:

Halve the pear, chop the kiwi fruit and greens, then juice all
ingredients alternately. Enjoy!

WATERMELON JUICE

Ingredients:

1 - 2 cups of watermelon
1 orange
1 green apple
1 kiwi fruit
1 cup kale or bok choy

Directions:

Cut skin off watermelon and orange, chop roughly. Chop kale and apple. Push everything into juicer alternating.

The End

NOTES

COPYRIGHT

Juice Recipes for Weight Loss:

Copyright © 2014 by Peggy Annear

Printed in Great Britain
by Amazon

61619175R00037